OH NO IT ISN'T!

RENARD PRESS — PLAYSCRIPT IX

OH NO IT ISN'T!:
FIRST PRODUCED BY LKT PRODUCTIONS IN 2018,
DIRECTED BY KENNEDY BLOOMER AND TOBY HAMPTON.
MR CHANCERY PLAYED BY ROBBIE CAPALDI,
MR WORTH PLAYED BY LUKE ADAMSON.

BY THE SAME WRITER:

ONE LAST WALTZ

PLAYSCRIPT VI

9781804470275

OH NO IT ISN'T!

LUKE ADAMSON

RENARD PRESS

RENARD PRESS LTD

124 City Road
London EC1V 2NX
United Kingdom
info@renardpress.com
020 8050 2928

www.renardpress.com

Oh No It Isn't! first published by Renard Press Ltd in 2023

Text © Luke Adamson, 2023
Cover design by Will Dady

Printed in the United Kingdom by Severn

ISBN: 978-1-80447-106-7

9 8 7 6 5 4 3 2 1

Luke Adamson asserts his right to be identified as the author of this work in accordance with the Copyright, Designs and Patents Act 1988.

This is a work of fiction. Any resemblance to actual persons, living or dead, is purely coincidental.

All rights reserved. This publication may not be reproduced, stored in a retrieval system or transmitted, in any form or by any means – electronic, mechanical, photocopying, recording or otherwise – without the prior permission of the publisher.

Renard Press is proud to be a climate positive publisher, meaning we take more carbon out of the air than we put in. For more information see renardpress.com/eco

Permission for producing this play may be applied for via the publisher, using the contact details above, or by emailing rights@renardpress.com.

CONTENTS

Oh No It Isn't!   7
  Notes   9
  Characters   9

  Preset   11

  Act One   13

  Act Two   33

  Act Three   47

OH NO IT ISN'T!

NOTES

The play takes place during the final night of a pantomime in a moth-eaten regional theatre. The action occurs both onstage and in the dressing room of Mr Chancery and Mr Worth. The changes between locations should be instant and indicated with lighting. As the onstage scenes are pantomime there is room for ad-libbing within character and playing with the audience, providing all the scripted lines are said. There should be no ad-libbing at all in the offstage scenes.

Despite being set in the world of pantomime, this is a play for a grown-up audience and contains adult language and themes.

CHARACTERS

MR CHANCERY: An excitable, up-and-coming actor with a somewhat uncontrollable energy.

MR WORTH: A more experienced, dedicated actor with a passion for the world of theatre.

PRESET

MR WORTH *is offstage.* MR CHANCERY *is sitting at his dressing table, doing his make-up, reading* Twelfth Night. *The show relay plays the sound of the audience entering the theatre, excitedly chattering.*
  After a time:

VOICEOVER (STAGE MANAGER): Ladies and gentlemen of the *Cinderella* company, this is your five-minute call; this is your five-minute call; you have five minutes. Thank you.

(MR WORTH *enters in frock and full make-up. He is carrying a mobile phone, which he places down on his dressing table in a temper. He takes a moment to brace himself and breathes deeply, swallows, breathes deeply again before launching into an elaborate vocal warm-up, featuring scales and tongue twisters.*)

VOICEOVER: Ladies and gentlemen of the *Cinderella* company, this is your act-one beginners call; all act-one beginners to the stage, please; this is your act-one beginners call.

(MR WORTH *checks his wig and make-up in the mirror, then looks at* MR CHANCERY, *who puts his book down and quickly checks his appearance. They walk together to the back, and pause in a pose. They turn and we're off.*)

ACT ONE

Part 1 – *The Show*

The 'sisters', MR WORTH and MR CHANCERY, sing a jazzy duet and take the opportunity to interact with the audience through the lyrics. The original production licensed the use of 'Sisters' by Irving Berlin.
The lights change and we're back in the dressing room.

MR WORTH (*taking his wig off*): I can't believe you were fucking out again.
MR CHANCERY: I was not out.
MR WORTH: You were out – you miss the entrance every time.
MR CHANCERY: You're coming in too early – you're ahead of the fucking track.
MR WORTH: You're dragging the tempo.
MR CHANCERY: You're impossible.

(*They continue their change.*)

MR WORTH: I can't believe they asked you back.
MR CHANCERY: It's what the audience want!
MR WORTH: Your jokes have been doing the rounds longer than I have.

MR CHANCERY: Well, if it ain't broke…
MR WORTH: At least you're back in a frock this year – what were they thinking casting you as the prince last year?
MR CHANCERY: Sleeping Beauty needs a prince.
MR WORTH: Yeah! A fucking handsome prince. A George Clooney lookalike, a make-the-mums-swoon-and-the-dads-jealous prince. Not the lovechild of John Cleese and Mr Fucking Tickle.
MR CHANCERY: Just shut up and undo this for me.

(MR WORTH *undoes* MR CHANCERY*'s frock and vice versa.*)

MR WORTH: Oh, they've done a good job on these this year – the stitching's lovely.
MR CHANCERY: And the attention to detail.
MR WORTH: Was it a new designer?
MR CHANCERY: I don't think so.
MR WORTH: Still Audrey?
MR CHANCERY: Yeah.
MR WORTH: Isn't she about ninety now?
MR CHANCERY: Seventy-five, she said.
MR WORTH: Seventy-five my arse.
MR CHANCERY: That's what she said.
MR WORTH: She's been seventy-five for the six years I've been here.
MR CHANCERY: Well, either way she's done a good job.
MR WORTH: Yeah, it's lovely fabric.
MR CHANCERY: Yeah.

(*Pause.*)

ACT ONE

MR CHANCERY: What were we talking about?
MR WORTH: Can't remember.

(*Pause.*)

MR WORTH: You know, I've never asked you your favourite.
MR CHANCERY: My favourite what?
MR WORTH: Panto.
MR CHANCERY: *Aladdin*.
MR WORTH: Ah, yeah.
MR CHANCERY: You?
MR WORTH: *Jack and the Beanstalk*.
MR CHANCERY: Fair enough.
MR WORTH: Least favourite?
MR CHANCERY: *Cinderella*.
MR WORTH: What? Really?
MR CHANCERY: Yeah.
MR WORTH: Why?
MR CHANCERY: No decent dame part.
MR WORTH: Er, what?
MR CHANCERY: Well, you know what I mean.
MR WORTH: You don't like sharing the dame part, you mean?
MR CHANCERY: Oh, give it a rest.
MR WORTH: You hate that you have to share the limelight with someone else.
MR CHANCERY: It's got nothing to do with that.
MR WORTH: You've always hated sharing the stage with me.
MR CHANCERY: Rubbish!
MR WORTH: You have.
MR CHANCERY: Nonsense.

MR WORTH: Ever since *Babes in the Wood*.
MR CHANCERY: Look—
MR WORTH: You haven't been the same since then.
MR CHANCERY: We agreed—
MR WORTH: You can't let it drop.
MR CHANCERY: *I* can't let it drop? You're the one that brings it up. Every year. Without fail. Move on.
MR WORTH: Move on?
MR CHANCERY: Move on.
MR WORTH: I'd love to, but you keep letting it get in the way.
MR CHANCERY: I let it get in the way?
MR WORTH: Well, clearly.
MR CHANCERY: I wasn't the one that requested a separate dressing room this year.
MR WORTH: Well. You weren't supposed to know about that, were you.
MR CHANCERY: Yeah, well. Walls have ears.
MR WORTH: Well, if we'd have had separate dressing rooms we wouldn't be arguing all the time, would we?
MR CHANCERY: No, but you couldn't get into that finale frock on your own.
MR WORTH: How'd you find out, anyway?
MR CHANCERY: I have my sources.
MR WORTH: Who? That's breach of confidence.
MR CHANCERY: Oh fuck off.
MR WORTH: No, seriously. My contract negotiations are my business – how did you find that out?
MR CHANCERY: Look, it's panto, word gets round.
MR WORTH: I'm fucking livid.
MR CHANCERY: What's next?

ACT ONE

MR WORTH: Hovel scene.
MR CHANCERY: Oh.

(*Pause; they continue to change into their hovel-scene outfits.*)

MR CHANCERY: Needs more gags.
MR WORTH: Needs new gags.
MR CHANCERY: Oh, here we go again.
MR WORTH: What?
MR CHANCERY: You can't just let it go, can you?
MR WORTH: Let what go? I'm just saying—
MR CHANCERY: You're like a stuck record!
MR WORTH: I'm just saying that some of those gags have been doing the rounds...
BOTH: Since my granddad was a child.
MR CHANCERY: I know.
MR WORTH: Well, it's true.
MR CHANCERY: You're just jealous that I get more laughs than you.
MR WORTH: It's got nothing to do with laughs – I just think—
MR CHANCERY: What's your least favourite?
MR WORTH: What?
MR CHANCERY: Your least favourite panto?
MR WORTH: Oh. *Puss in Boots*.
MR CHANCERY: Why?
MR WORTH: Because it's fucking shite.

(*Lights change; they're back on stage.*)

MR WORTH: Hello, girls and boys! (*Waits for response, ad-libs with audience.*)

MR CHANCERY: Rumour has it that the prince is coming round to hand out invitations to the royal ball, and we're going to snare him without him even realising.

MR WORTH: We're going to be so alarming.

MR CHANCERY: Alluring.

MR WORTH: That's what I said. We're going to harm him with our wiles.

MR CHANCERY: Charm him with our smiles.

MR WORTH: That's what I said. Then marry him and live happily every after.

MR CHANCERY: Marry him and live happily ever after.

MR WORTH: Sorry, yes, you're right. Marry him and live happily ever after.

MR CHANCERY: Well, I am.

MR WORTH: No, I am!

MR CHANCERY: When he sees me he won't be able to contain himself.

MR WORTH: Yes, I'm sure he'll be positively frothing with anticipation.

MR CHANCERY: I'll look like a million dollars.

MR WORTH: Yes – green and crinkled. He won't even notice you, because I'll look like a movie star.

MR CHANCERY: Yes. Shrek.

MR WORTH: You're just jealous because I'm so sexy.

MR CHANCERY: You think you're sexy?

MR WORTH: If anything I'm a bit too sexy!

MR CHANCERY: You think you're too sexy?

MR WORTH: Just a little bit *too* sexy.

MR CHANCERY: Well if you're too sexy then I'm... four sexy. (*Aside:*) That's more sexy.

MR WORTH: That doesn't even make sense.

ACT ONE

MR CHANCERY: No, but it's a great intro for a song!
MR WORTH: Hit it!

(*The sisters sing 'I'm Too Sexy' by Right Said Fred, modifying the lyrics as below.*)

MR CHANCERY: And I'm too sexy for Milan,
 Scunthorpe (*or local place name*) and Japan…
MR CHANCERY: Too sexy for your hat?
 It makes your neck look fat!
MR CHANCERY: I'm too sexy for my— (MR WORTH *shoves him out of the way.*)
MR WORTH: Too sexy for my— (MR CHANCERY *knocks him out and catches him.*)
BOTH: And we're too sexy for this show!

(*Lights change; we're back in the dressing room.* MR WORTH *and* MR CHANCERY *remove their hovel costumes during the following scene and change into slosh costumes.*)

MR WORTH: That routine is so dated.
MR CHANCERY: It just needs more before the number.
MR WORTH: It needs a different number.
MR CHANCERY: The song gets laughs.
MR WORTH: Oh, come on. Nobody under fifty knows Right Said Fred.
MR CHANCERY: Who?
MR WORTH: Right Said Fred.
MR CHANCERY: Yeah. Who?
MR WORTH: Are you kidding?
MR CHANCERY: No.

MR WORTH: Right Said Fred.
MR CHANCERY: Yeah, you just repeating it isn't really making it any clearer.
MR WORTH: They sang that song.
MR CHANCERY: Which song?
MR WORTH: That song. That fucking song. The one we just sang.
MR CHANCERY: Oh really?
MR WORTH: Give me strength.
MR CHANCERY: Why are you in such a foul mood?
MR WORTH: Foul mood?
MR CHANCERY: Yeah.
MR WORTH: You think I'm in a foul mood?
MR CHANCERY: Yeah, you've been as miserable as sin all night.
MR WORTH: Oh right, OK.
MR CHANCERY: What gives?
MR WORTH: Oh, I don't know. Maybe it's something to do with the fact that I've spent this entire season playing alongside an arrogant, talentless prick who tries to upstage me in every scene.
MR CHANCERY: Well, don't pull your punches, tell us how you really feel!
MR WORTH: An untrained amateur who has slept his way into every job he's ever had.
MR CHANCERY: Man's gotta work.
MR WORTH: Who wouldn't know real acting if it slapped him in the face.
MR CHANCERY: And how many *Dr Who*s have you done?
MR WORTH: This is exactly what I mean! You only got that job because you slept with the producer!

ACT ONE

MR CHANCERY: Associate producer.

MR WORTH: Exactly.

MR CHANCERY: And they had nothing to do with the casting.

MR WORTH: I've been here longer than you, and yet your name has somehow ended up above mine on the poster.

MR CHANCERY: Well it's clearly what the punters want.

MR WORTH: You have no technique, your voice is substandard and your accent's all over the place.

MR CHANCERY: For fuck's sake, it's only panto.

(*Pause.*)

MR WORTH: Fuck you.

MR CHANCERY: What?

MR WORTH: Fuck you.

MR CHANCERY: OK.

MR WORTH: You've no respect for me, you've no respect for your audience, you've no respect for the show.

MR CHANCERY: Mate, it's just a job.

MR WORTH: No respect. For the form.

MR CHANCERY: It's panto – you turn up, piss about and fuck off. That's it. They love it.

MR WORTH: You can't even get a simple spoonerism right.

MR CHANCERY: What're you talking about?

MR WORTH: Last year. Fairy Hucklebuck.

MR CHANCERY: Are you still going on about that?

MR WORTH: You went out in front of eight hundred people and shouted, 'Has anyone seen the hairy fucklebuck?'

MR CHANCERY: Yes, I remember. I was there.

MR WORTH: It's a family show, for Christ's sake!

MR CHANCERY: Made the local news. Doubled the audiences.
MR WORTH: You're so ignorant.
MR CHANCERY: It's a business, buddy. You've got to treat it as such. If you love it too much it'll kill you.
MR WORTH: Just... (*Sticks both middle fingers up at him.*)

(*Silence.*)

MR CHANCERY: Look, I know this gig means a lot to you.
MR WORTH: No you don't. You don't know the half of it.
MR CHANCERY: But you have your ways, and... I have my ways.
MR WORTH: Just stop. Stop talking.
MR CHANCERY: Fine.
MR WORTH: You've ruined this panto season for me.
MR CHANCERY: Well, I'm sorry about that.
MR WORTH: At least if I'd had my own dressing room I'd have had a bit of my own space.
MR CHANCERY: No room for egos in this game, mate.
MR WORTH: It's not about egos. It's about me getting away from you, it's about me having the space to... to...
MR CHANCERY: To what?
MR WORTH: Oh, fuck off.
MR CHANCERY: No, go on, I'm genuinely interested in what you have to say.
MR WORTH: Just... just... You know.
MR CHANCERY: No I don't. What?
MR WORTH: A fucking cupboard would have done. Just somewhere I could change away from you.

ACT ONE

MR CHANCERY: Well, if I'd have known you felt that strongly then I'd have said yes.

MR WORTH: What do you mean, said yes?

MR CHANCERY: When they asked me if I'd share with the chorus boys.

MR WORTH: When who asked you?

MR CHANCERY: Sarah.

MR WORTH: Box Office Sarah?

MR CHANCERY: Stage Manager Sarah.

MR WORTH: Stage Manager Sarah asked you if you wanted to share with the ensemble?

MR CHANCERY: Well, why would Box Office Sarah ask me about my dressing room?

MR WORTH: Stop being flippant. She asked you if you wanted to share with the ensemble?

MR CHANCERY: Yeah. I said no. Clearly.

MR WORTH: How come you got asked?

MR CHANCERY: What?

MR WORTH: How come you got asked which dressing room you wanted to be in? They never ask me.

MR CHANCERY: Well you're not sleeping with stage management, are you.

MR WORTH: Oh god! You're fucking Sarah?

MR CHANCERY: When I feel like it, yeah.

MR WORTH: I don't believe this!

MR CHANCERY: Weekends only, at the moment.

MR WORTH: Is there anyone in this company you haven't slept with?

MR CHANCERY: Most of the ensemble.

MR WORTH: Most?

MR CHANCERY: Yeah. Twiglets don't do it for me.

MR WORTH: And how do they all feel about it? Do they know about each other?
MR CHANCERY: Well, Josh and Lucy do, because they were there together.
MR WORTH: Oh my god.
MR CHANCERY: Love a threesome.
MR WORTH: Too much information there.
MR CHANCERY: Don't know about the rest.
MR WORTH: You really think you're God's gift, don't you?
MR CHANCERY: Not really. Just like sex.
MR WORTH: Have you ever actually loved someone? Like, really deeply had feelings for someone?
MR CHANCERY: What's that got to do with it?
MR WORTH: Well, I think it's got quite a lot to do with it!
MR CHANCERY: Well I... disagree.
MR WORTH: Course you do.

(Pause – the show relay has gone quiet.)

MR CHANCERY: Are we off?
MR WORTH: What?
MR CHANCERY: It's gone quiet – are we late?
MR WORTH: We can't be.
MR CHANCERY: It's gone really quiet – what's happening?
MR WORTH: She hasn't sung yet, has she?
MR CHANCERY: I don't think so.
MR WORTH: Shit – maybe you're right.
MR CHANCERY: Oh shit. Quick!

(They hurriedly put their wigs on and do up their frocks and tear out of the exit, just as the band strikes up and Cinderella sings.)

ACT ONE

MR WORTH: I told you she hadn't sung yet.

MR CHANCERY: Yes, well, we'd have known that if you hadn't have been prattling on about love and all that bollocks.

MR WORTH: It's not bollocks.

MR CHANCERY: No, these are bollocks. (*Grabs crotch.*)

MR WORTH: Oh, will you grow up!

MR CHANCERY: Grow up? (*Indicates to himself, pointing at his costume.*)

MR WORTH: Do you not realise that you could be really hurting people? Sleeping with them and dropping them without a word?

MR CHANCERY: Mate, it's panto – everybody knows what this is.

MR WORTH: Not necessarily.

MR CHANCERY: What?

MR WORTH: Just because you don't have feelings doesn't mean they don't.

MR CHANCERY: Well, more fool them.

MR WORTH: You're so selfish.

MR CHANCERY: Oh, I see.

MR WORTH: What do you see?

MR CHANCERY: That's what this is all about.

MR WORTH: What?

MR CHANCERY: My god, it's so obvious.

MR WORTH: What's so obvious?

MR CHANCERY: What this is about. Why you keep going on like this.

MR WORTH: What are you talking about?

MR CHANCERY: *Babes in the Wood*!

(*Lights chance and they're onstage.*)

MR WORTH: Hello, girls and boys! (*Waits for response. Room for ad-libbing here.*) We're very glad you're here, as we need help getting ready for the ball, don't we, darling sister?

MR CHANCERY: We certainly do – but first we need to find the bag with all the make-up in it.

MR WORTH: Ah yes, the old bag. (*Looks around the audience and finally at* MR CHANCERY.) Found it!

MR CHANCERY: Oh, boo to you. Can you see the bag, girls and boys? (*'Behind you!'*) Where is it? (*And so on.*)

(*They finally find the bag.*)

MR CHANCERY: Ah, yes! Here it is!

MR WORTH: It certainly is an old bag.

MR CHANCERY: Very old.

MR WORTH: Almost as old as you.

MR CHANCERY: How dare you! I'm not a minute older than you.

MR WORTH: No, only fifty-seven seconds older.

MR CHANCERY: And I hide it well.

MR WORTH: Well, that's all the Botox.

MR CHANCERY: Oh, don't talk about Santa's little helper! Where is that bag from, anyway?

MR WORTH: This bag? Well, it used to belong to Daddy.

MR CHANCERY: It's Dad's bag?

MR WORTH: That's right – it's Dad's bag.

MR CHANCERY: Ah yes, I remember! It's Dad's bag.

MR WORTH: Yep, definitely Dad's bag.

MR CHANCERY: And where did he get it from?

ACT ONE

MR WORTH: ...Baghdad.

MR CHANCERY: Baghdad?

MR WORTH: Yes, Baghdad.

MR CHANCERY: Did Dad get that bag in Baghdad?

MR WORTH: Dad did get this bag in Baghdad.

MR CHANCERY: Did he?

MR WORTH: Diddy? I suppose he was never that tall.

MR CHANCERY: So. Did diddy Dad get that bag in Baghdad?

MR WORTH: Diddy dad did get this bag in Baghdad.

MR CHANCERY: It's quite a big bag, isn't it?

MR WORTH: Compared to diddy Dad it's a big bag, yes.

MR CHANCERY: So did diddy Dad get that big bag in Baghdad, did diddy Dad?

MR WORTH: Diddy Dad did get this big bag in Baghdad, diddy Dad did.

MR CHANCERY: It's a bit baggy, isn't it?

MR WORTH: I suppose it is quite baggy, yes.

MR CHANCERY: So...

MR WORTH: Brace yourselves!

MR CHANCERY: Did diddy Dad get that bit-baggy big bag in Baghdad, did diddy Dad?

MR WORTH: Sorry, what?

MR CHANCERY: So did diddy Dad get that bit-baggy big bag in Baghdad, did diddy Dad?

MR WORTH: One more time.

MR CHANCERY: So did diddy Dad get that bit-baggy big bag in Baghdad, did diddy Dad?

MR WORTH (*inhales deeply in preparation*): Yes.

MR CHANCERY: Well, get it open, and let's do our make-up for the ball!

MR WORTH: I'm so excited!

MR CHANCERY: What have we here then? (*Removing props from the bag.*) Face wash.

MR WORTH: Oh, goody.

MR CHANCERY: Face cream.

MR WORTH: Oh, goody goody.

MR CHANCERY: Corn plasters.

MR WORTH: Oh good— Corn plasters?

MR CHANCERY: Yes. In case the corn gets hurt.

MR WORTH (*under his breath*): Six weeks and that's never got a laugh.

MR CHANCERY: And to finish, a nice powder puff.

MR WORTH: Oh, goody goody goody.

MR CHANCERY: Who's going first?

MR WORTH: Shall I go first?

MR CHANCERY: What if I want to go first?

MR WORTH: Let's flip for it. Do you have a coin?

MR CHANCERY: Yes. Here! (*Pulls out coin.*)

MR WORTH: Great! (*Takes coin and pockets it.*) OK, you can go first.

MR CHANCERY: Oh, must be my lucky day. (*They set up for the slosh routine.*)

MR WORTH: So first off, let's wash your face nice and clean with lots of face wash. (*Pumps lots of facewash on to* MR CHANCERY*'s face.*)

MR CHANCERY: Oh, thank you.

MR WORTH: Oh, I mustn't forget to rub it in. (*Rubs it quite vigorously.*)

MR CHANCERY: Ow! Blimey! You're really getting in there today, aren't you, darling sister?

ACT ONE

MR WORTH: Well, we want to make sure you're nice and clean to meet the prince!

MR CHANCERY: Though I don't think you need to wash me quite so hard!

MR WORTH: All done. Now it's time to wash it all off! (*Bucket/soda squirter to wash it off; soaks him.*)

MR CHANCERY: Ah that's better! How do I look?

MR WORTH: Oh, you look radiant!

MR CHANCERY: Do I?

MR WORTH: Oh yes.

MR CHANCERY: Nobody has ever told me I look radiant before.

MR WORTH: Oh no, sorry, not radiant – what's that word? Sounds like radiant. Radiator! You look like a radiator!

MR CHANCERY (*under his breath*): Yeah, cause that's hilarious.

MR WORTH: Next up, the face cream!

MR CHANCERY: Oh yes! What is it? Oil of Olay?

MR WORTH: No.

MR CHANCERY: Ah, is it the Spanish version? Oil of Olé?

MR WORTH: No, I think it's French. It says Oil On-Zhee-Nay.

MR CHANCERY: Ooh, Oil On-Zhee-Nay. Sounds lovely – slather it on!

MR WORTH (*slathering thick black oil over* MR CHANCERY*'s face*): Here we go!

MR CHANCERY: Blimey, is it meant to be that colour?

MR WORTH: Well, I assume so...

MR CHANCERY: Pass me that bottle!

MR WORTH: I want you to really reap the benefits! I'll put some more on! (*Pours more on before passing the bottle to* MR CHANCERY.)

MR CHANCERY: On-Zhee-Nay? ON-ZHEE-NAY?! That doesn't say On-Zhee-Nay, it says Engine! You've put engine oil on my face!

MR WORTH: Whoops! Sorry, sister dear! Let me wash it off for you! (*More soda/water.*)

MR CHANCERY: Oh, I feel like a fireman has unleashed his hose on me.

MR WORTH: I'd love to have a fireman unleash his hose on me!

MR CHANCERY: How do I look?

MR WORTH: Just one final finishing touch!

MR CHANCERY: Oh? And what's that?

MR WORTH: A bit of powder.

MR CHANCERY: Oh yes, powder!

MR WORTH: Are you ready?

MR CHANCERY: As I'll ever be!

MR WORTH: Here we are, sister dear! Three... two... one... (*Swings a full powder puff and catches* MR CHANCERY *square in the face. Lights. Backstage.*)

MR CHANCERY: What the fuck was that?

MR WORTH: What?

MR CHANCERY: That!

MR WORTH: That was the slapstick routine. Same as I've always done it.

MR CHANCERY: You nearly broke my fucking nose!

MR WORTH: Oh, stop moaning.

MR CHANCERY: And you put twice as much of the oil on.

MR WORTH: They were loving it – it's what they wanted!

MR CHANCERY: Stick to the routine!

MR WORTH: You know as well as I do that the routine is old and tired. They've seen it a hundred times before – I'm just trying to keep it exciting.

ACT ONE

MR CHANCERY: You're impossible.

MR WORTH: Well, it's the interval next – you've plenty of time to redo your make-up. I'm going for a coffee. (*Leaves.*)

MR CHANCERY: Fucking amateur.

(MR CHANCERY *removes what's left of his make-up and starts to retouch it. The lights dim and the audience can be heard enjoying the break over the relay.*)

ACT TWO

Part 2 – The Show

MR CHANCERY *is sitting at his desk touching up the last of his make-up.* MR WORTH *enters, coffee in hand.*

MR WORTH: I think I owe you an apology.
MR CHANCERY: You think?
MR WORTH: Yes, I think.
MR CHANCERY: Go on, then.
MR WORTH: I'm sorry.
MR CHANCERY: That it?
MR WORTH: What?
MR CHANCERY: Is that it?
MR WORTH: What do you mean?
MR CHANCERY: I just thought there might be more to it than that.
MR WORTH: Well, what do you want me to say?
MR CHANCERY: 'I'm sorry for almost breaking your fucking nose' would be a start.
MR WORTH: I'm sorry for almost breaking your nose.
MR CHANCERY: Fucking nose.
MR WORTH: Fucking nose.
MR CHANCERY: I'm sorry for going off track…

MR WORTH: I'm sorry for going off track.
MR CHANCERY: And breaking the first rule of the Ugly Sisters...
MR WORTH: What's that?
MR CHANCERY: To ad-lib with the intention of belittling one's sister.
MR WORTH: Ah. I'm sorry for breaking the first rule of the Ugly Sisters.
MR CHANCERY: And I'm sorry for being a fucking amateur.
MR WORTH: What?
MR CHANCERY: I'm sorry for being a fucking amateur.
MR WORTH: You're taking the piss now?
MR CHANCERY: *I'm* taking the piss? You nearly broke my nose with a powder puff!
MR WORTH: Don't call me an amateur.
MR CHANCERY: Well, it was pretty fucking amateur.
MR WORTH: DON'T CALL ME AN AMATEUR.
MR CHANCERY: All right, calm down.
MR WORTH: Take it back.
MR CHANCERY: What?
MR WORTH: Take it back.
MR CHANCERY: I don't believe this.
MR WORTH: Take it back!
MR CHANCERY: You're the one that went off track and behaved badly, and you're annoyed at me?
MR WORTH: TAKE IT BACK!
MR CHANCERY: Jesus Christ, OK, OK. I take it back – you're not an amateur.
MR WORTH: Thank you.
MR CHANCERY: You're just a twat.

ACT TWO

(*Pause.*)

MR WORTH: Yeah, that's fair.

(*Pause.*)

MR WORTH: I'm just going through a lot of stuff at the moment.
MR CHANCERY: Right.
MR WORTH: I don't really feel like going into it.
MR CHANCERY: I didn't ask you to.
MR WORTH: Sure.

(*Pause.*)

VOICEOVER (STAGE MANAGER): This is your call, please, Mr Chancery and Mr Worth – Mr Chancery and Mr Worth, your calls, please, thank you.

(MR WORTH *and* MR CHANCERY *begin to change into their ballroom outfits.* MR CHANCERY *has an easier time of it than* MR WORTH *and ends up helping* MR WORTH *into it. There is a moment of acceptance from* MR WORTH.)

MR CHANCERY: You know, I think this has to be one of the weakest ballroom scenes I've done.
MR WORTH: Really?
MR CHANCERY: Yeah. I mean, it has all the necessary plot points, but it's pretty dull otherwise.
MR WORTH: I suppose.
MR CHANCERY: Oh well. Only have to do it once more.

MR WORTH: Thank god.
MR CHANCERY: You ready?
MR WORTH: As I'll ever be.

(*Lights change – onstage.*)

MR WORTH: Oh, the prince is coming, sister dear!
MR CHANCERY: I'm so excited! I've put my best eyelashes on for the occasion.
MR WORTH: Hmm. Just a shame you put them on the dog. Ooh! Here he comes! Now remember, sister dear, on occasions like this first impressions are very important!
MR CHANCERY: Of course. I've been practising.
MR WORTH: OK, let me see.
MR CHANCERY: OK, here goes. (*Leaping towards imaginary prince:*) PRINCEY!
MR WORTH: Woah woah woah.
MR CHANCERY: Too much?
MR WORTH: Just a bit. You need to be more casual. Try this. (*Turns away, glances in direction of prince, raises one eyebrow:*) Hey. (*Turns away again.*)
MR CHANCERY: That might be a bit too casual.
MR WORTH: Oh.
MR CHANCERY: Perhaps we should just stand and look cool.
MR WORTH: Good idea.

(MR CHANCERY *leans against a nearby wall.*)

MR WORTH: Nice.

ACT TWO

(MR WORTH *also leans against it, at a more acute angle.* MR CHANCERY *leans more acutely.* MR WORTH *leans more acutely still. Soon they're almost horizontal.*)

MR WORTH: This is ridiculous.

MR CHANCERY: Speak for yourself – I look hot.

MR WORTH: I know – I can see the sweat marks in your armpit.

MR CHANCERY: Oh, how dare you. I'm a lady! I don't sweat! I glow.

MR WORTH: In that case you're glowing like a pig.

MR CHANCERY: Perhaps we should just dance.

MR WORTH: Good idea.

(MR CHANCERY *dances.*)

MR WORTH: What on earth's that?!

MR CHANCERY: It's my dance.

MR WORTH: It's ridiculous. That's not how you dance! This is how you dance!

(MR WORTH *dances too.*)

MR CHANCERY: It looks like you've got something up your bottom.

MR WORTH: Well, it looks like you've got something coming out of yours!

MR CHANCERY: Well, let's see which one the prince prefers.

(*They continue to dance ridiculously, trying to outdo each other, before the lights change – back in the dressing room.* MR WORTH *sits and picks up a crossword he's clearly been working on for the whole run.*)

MR CHANCERY: Barely a titter.
MR WORTH: It's not a great routine.
MR CHANCERY: It was getting laughs at the start of the run.
MR WORTH: Well it's you – you've started pushing it.
MR CHANCERY: What?
MR WORTH: You're pushing it. Your dance is too much now – that's why nobody's laughing, you're just making the audience uncomfortable.
MR CHANCERY: I'm pushing it?
MR WORTH: Yeah.
MR CHANCERY: I'm just trying to make up for your lack of enthusiasm.
MR WORTH: Lack of enthusiasm?
MR CHANCERY: Yeah.
MR WORTH: I'm doing it exactly the same as I always have.
MR CHANCERY: Rubbish! You can't be arsed any more.
MR WORTH: I can't be arsed?
MR CHANCERY: Yeah.
MR WORTH: That's rich! At least I've never sent the understudy on because of a hangover.
MR CHANCERY: I've told you before, that was a stomach bug!
MR WORTH: On New Year's Day? Pull the other one!
MR CHANCERY: I was vomiting everywhere.
MR WORTH: Yeah. Hangover. You were fine the next day.
MR CHANCERY: Yeah – a twenty-four-hour stomach bug.
MR WORTH: Whatever.

(*Pause.*)

MR CHANCERY: Could have been food poisoning.
MR WORTH: Oh really? Could it?

MR CHANCERY: Yeah.
MR WORTH: I thought it was a stomach bug?
MR CHANCERY: Could have been either.
MR WORTH: Could have been a hangover.
MR CHANCERY: I barely had anything to drink on New Year's Eve.
MR WORTH: You were put into a taxi at 6 a.m.
MR CHANCERY: That's not how I remember it.
MR WORTH: I'm not surprised – you were unconscious.
MR CHANCERY: Stop exaggerating. I may have had a nap...
MR WORTH: Exaggerating? You threw up on the work-experience kid and passed out in the prop store.
MR CHANCERY: Not my finest hour.
MR WORTH: You can say that again.
MR CHANCERY: Not my finest—

(MR WORTH *stops* MR CHANCERY *with a glare. Pause.*)

MR CHANCERY: And to get a stomach bug the next day is really bad luck.
MR WORTH: It was a fucking hangover!
MR CHANCERY: Let's agree to disagree.
MR WORTH: Jesus Christ.

(*Pause.*)

MR CHANCERY: What you doing?
MR WORTH: Crossword.
MR CHANCERY: Oh. How you doing?
MR WORTH: Yeah, fine thanks.
MR CHANCERY: Need any help?

MR WORTH: No, thank you.
MR CHANCERY: You sure?
MR WORTH: OK, yeah, fine. Here's one: three letters – something, A, T. The clue is: Not a dog.
MR CHANCERY (*thinks, then*): Mat.
MR WORTH: What?
MR CHANCERY: Mat.
MR WORTH: Mat?
MR CHANCERY: Yeah.
MR WORTH: Mat?
MR CHANCERY: Yeah, like a doormat.
MR WORTH: You're kidding?
MR CHANCERY: No.
MR WORTH: Mat?
MR CHANCERY: Well, it's not a dog, is it?
MR WORTH: No, I suppose not.
MR CHANCERY: And it fits.
MR WORTH: Technically.
MR CHANCERY: Need help with any others?
MR WORTH: No.
MR CHANCERY: You sure?
MR WORTH: Yep.

(*Pause.*)

MR CHANCERY: That wasn't a real clue, was it?
MR WORTH: How did you guess?
MR CHANCERY: Well, you didn't write it in.
MR WORTH: Of course. Nothing gets past you, does it, Poirot?
MR CHANCERY: Are you sure you're all right?
MR WORTH: Yes… I'm fine!

ACT TWO

(*Lights change – they're onstage.*)

MR CHANCERY: Oh, he's nearly here!
MR WORTH: He's nearly here?
MR CHANCERY: I'm so excited!
MR WORTH: I'm so excited!
MR CHANCERY: One of us is going to marry the prince!

(*Pause.*)

I said one of us is going to marry the prince!
MR WORTH: Erm, yes! One of us is going to marry the prince!
MR CHANCERY: I can't wait to put my foot in the crystal slipper!

(MR WORTH *stares off into the distance.*)

I said I can't wait to put my foot in the crystal slipper!
MR WORTH: Sorry?
MR CHANCERY: What's wrong with you, sis? Are you nervous about meeting the prince? (*Under his breath:*) Pull it together!
MR WORTH: Yes, sorry. What were you saying?
MR CHANCERY: Well I for one can't wait to put my foot in the crystal slipper!
MR WORTH: Your big feet wouldn't even fit in the Crystal Palace!

(*Lights change to blues – the wings.*)

MR CHANCERY (*shouting*): What are you playing at?
MR WORTH: I'm trying, OK!
MR CHANCERY: Get it together!
MR WORTH: I will!
MR CHANCERY: You made me look a mug out there!
MR WORTH: I'll sort it out!
MR CHANCERY: You'd better!

(*Lights – onstage.*)

MR WORTH: It's song-sheet time, girls and boys!
MR CHANCERY: Your favourite part of the show!
MR WORTH: Well, it's certainly our favourite part of the show!
MR CHANCERY: Oh sis, I feel something coming on.
MR WORTH: Oh no! Do you need your pills?
MR CHANCERY: No, I feel like it's time for a big reveal!
MR WORTH: Erm… I'm not sure it's that kind of show!
MR CHANCERY: There's something I've kept rolled up and tucked away, and I want to unfurl it in front of this audience!
MR WORTH: It's definitely not that kind of show!
MR CHANCERY: I'm talking about the song sheet!!
MR WORTH: Oh of course! The song sheet!
MR CHANCERY: So let's build the tension – everybody put your hands on your legs and give us a drum roll please! Stamp your feet! Here we go!

(*The song sheet is revealed. It's a pathetic moment – perhaps a lone party popper erupts.*)

ACT TWO

MR CHANCERY: Oh, what an anti-climax.

MR WORTH: It's usually much later in the evening before she's saying that!

MR CHANCERY: OK! So! We'll sing the song through first so you can hear how it goes, and then you can all join in! OK?

MR WORTH: Here goes!

Some like a cuddle in the moonlight...

MR CHANCERY: Some like a cuddle in the dark...

MR WORTH: Some like a cuddle in an old armchair...

MR CHANCERY: Some like a cuddle in the park...

MR WORTH: Some like a cuddle in the cowshed... (*Moos.*)

MR CHANCERY: Some like a cuddle in a flat...

BOTH: But give me a cuddle with a nice young man on Ilkley Moor Bah Tat!

MR WORTH: Great stuff! So what we're going to do now, madam (*singling out an audience member*), what we're going to do now is split you in two!

MR CHANCERY: Woah woah woah! You can't do that! It's not Penn and Teller!

MR WORTH: I'm talking about the audience! We're going to split the audience into two teams!

MR CHANCERY: Oh right, I see!

MR WORTH: This side of the audience are my team. We'll be Team One!

MR CHANCERY: And this side of the audience are my team. We'll be Team Thundercats.

MR WORTH (*giving* MR CHANCERY *a look*): OK... Well, Team One, we'll sing lines one, three and five.

MR CHANCERY: And Team Thundercats will sing lines two, four and...? (*Prompts audience to reply,* 'SIX!') Great!

MR WORTH: And then we'll all come together to sing the last two lines. OK?
MR CHANCERY: Ooh, I do love it when we come together. Great stuff. Here we go, then. After you, sis!
MR WORTH: OK, here we go! One, two, three, four... Some like a cuddle in the moonlight...
MR CHANCERY: Some like a cuddle in the dark...
MR WORTH: Some like a cuddle in an old armchair...
MR CHANCERY: Some like a cuddle in the park...
MR WORTH: Some like a...

(*He stops. The song might carry on for a second or so until* MR CHANCERY *realises that* MR WORTH *has stopped and seems to be struggling.*)

MR CHANCERY: Are you OK, sis? How can you have forgotten the words? They're written up there!
MR WORTH: Erm... Oh, sorry, yes! Erm. I just had a funny turn.
MR CHANCERY (*trying to cover*): Funny turn? I'll show you a funny turn! (*Does a funny turn.*)
MR WORTH: Sorry – where were we?
MR CHANCERY: Shall we just skip to the competition?
MR WORTH: Er, yes... competition – great idea! OK, so, Team One, it's us versus them and the loudest team wins – we've been doing this all Christmas and, well, I've never won, so let's really go for it, OK? Really loud!
MR CHANCERY: Thundercats, let's just have some fun, OK!
MR WORTH: All right, Team One, are you ready? (*Prompts audience response.*)

ACT TWO

MR CHANCERY: Team Thundercats, are you ready? (*Prompts response.*)

MR WORTH: OK, Team One, here we go! Nice and loud… One, two, three, four… Some like a cuddle in the moonlight. LOUDER!

(MR WORTH *slowly becomes manic, shouting constantly at the audience to sing louder. He is losing control.*)

MR CHANCERY: Some like a cuddle in the dark. Great stuff!

MR WORTH: Some like a cuddle in an old armchair. COME ON, LOUDER!

MR CHANCERY: Some like a cuddle in the park. We're winning!

MR WORTH: Some like a cuddle in the cowshed! SING UP!

MR CHANCERY: Some like a cuddle in a flat…

MR WORTH: SING, YOU CUNTS!

(MR WORTH *freezes in horrific realisation of what he has done. Blackout.*)

ACT THREE

Part 3 – Post Show

In the darkness we hear the final strains of 'We'll Meet Again' over the show relay, followed by rapturous applause and shouts of 'Encore!' Eventually the applause dies down and is followed by audience murmurs, which in turns dies out. We hear the FRONT-OF-HOUSE MANAGER *over the relay:*

VOICEOVER (HOUSE MANAGER): House clear!

(*The lights come up in the dressing room and we find* MR CHANCERY *sitting at his dressing table dressed in his civvies, checking his phone.* MR WORTH *enters, still in full costume, though it is half hanging off; his wig is askew and his make-up is smudged down his face from where he has clearly been crying. He stands in the doorway. There is a pause.*)

MR WORTH: That's it, then.
MR CHANCERY: Yep.
MR WORTH: All over for another year.
MR CHANCERY: Uh-huh.
MR WORTH: Ticket sales were slightly down this year.
MR CHANCERY: Really?
MR WORTH: Yeah.

MR CHANCERY: Well, they're making them too expensive.

MR WORTH: I suppose.

MR CHANCERY: Costs a family of four nearly a hundred and fifty quid just for the tickets – it's too much.

MR WORTH: Especially if you factor in a four-pound programme, sweets and ice creams.

MR CHANCERY: And a cheeky gin and tonic.

MR WORTH: That's another seven pound fifty.

MR CHANCERY: No wonder ticket sales are down.

MR WORTH: Especially when they can sit at home and watch Michael McIntyre for nothing.

MR CHANCERY: I've never seen the appeal.

MR WORTH: Me neither. They need to be careful, though.

MR CHANCERY: Who?

MR WORTH: The theatre.

MR CHANCERY: Why?

MR WORTH: Well, they don't want to drive the panto crowd away by making the tickets too expensive. Keeps this place afloat the rest of the year.

MR CHANCERY: Yeah. I don't suppose the plays of Stanistrivsky pack them in in quite the same way.

MR WORTH: Most people come to the theatre once a year for their annual gigglefest and then forget the place exists.

MR CHANCERY: Sign of the times, I suppose.

MR WORTH: Fewer theatres producing their own work, fewer jobs for actors.

MR CHANCERY: And you're more likely to be cast if you've been on bloody *Love Island* than if you've been to drama school.

MR WORTH: What a fucking shitshow.

MR CHANCERY: Yeah.

ACT THREE

(*There is another pause as* MR WORTH *takes off his wig and frock.* MR CHANCERY *just sits there.*)

MR WORTH: You're ready quickly.
MR CHANCERY: I've got people to meet.
MR WORTH: Family?
MR CHANCERY: Agent.
MR WORTH: Oh, nice.
MR CHANCERY: Yeah. They like to make the effort.
MR WORTH: Haven't they seen it already?
MR CHANCERY: Yeah, press night.
MR WORTH: Yeah.
MR CHANCERY: Has your agent seen it?
MR WORTH: No, they… don't really like panto.
MR CHANCERY: Oh, right.
MR WORTH: I don't think they understand it, to be honest.
MR CHANCERY: Are they local?
MR WORTH: No – London.
MR CHANCERY: Well, it is a bit of a trek.
MR WORTH: Yours has been twice, so it can't be that hard.
MR CHANCERY: I suppose.

(*Another lull in the conversation.*)

MR CHANCERY: I should go meet them, then.
MR WORTH: Yeah, don't let me hold you up.

(MR CHANCERY *wants to say something but thinks better of it, grabs his bag and heads to leave.*)

MR WORTH: I've got a bottle if you fancy a glass?

MR CHANCERY: Erm...
MR WORTH: It is tradition.
MR CHANCERY: Yeah, sure.

(MR WORTH *takes bottle from his bag and* MR CHANCERY *finds two mugs.*)

MR WORTH: Always raise a glass on the last night.
MR CHANCERY: What is it?
MR WORTH: Red wine.
MR CHANCERY: Yeah, I can see that. What type?
MR WORTH (*studying label*): Just says 'red wine'.
MR CHANCERY: Ah, classy.
MR WORTH: £3.50 from Aldi.
MR CHANCERY: Right.
MR WORTH: Says it goes well with red meats and cheeses.
MR CHANCERY: Perfect.
MR WORTH: Haven't got either of those, but it's good to know.
MR CHANCERY: Yeah, I suppose.

(*In silence* MR WORTH *pours two mugs full.*)

MR CHANCERY: Cheers.
MR WORTH: Yeah, cheers.
MR CHANCERY: To *Cinderella*.
MR WORTH: To *Cinderella*, and all who sailed in her. (*Drinks.*)
MR CHANCERY: I did. (*Drinks.*)
MR WORTH (*spitting out his wine*): Oh, for god's sake!
MR CHANCERY: After the company curry night.
MR WORTH: I don't know why it still surprises me.

ACT THREE

MR CHANCERY: She's filth.

MR WORTH: Is there anyone you wouldn't sleep with?

MR CHANCERY: Well, like I said, twiglets aren't really my thing, but I'm not fussy.

MR WORTH: Clearly.

MR CHANCERY: Male, female, dolphin. Anything with a pulse.

MR WORTH: I meant what I said earlier. You'll hurt people.

MR CHANCERY: Ah, chances are I'll never see them again.

MR WORTH: You might.

MR CHANCERY: Meh.

(They drink.)

MR WORTH: You got anything lined up?

MR CHANCERY: Yeah, a rep season in Canterbury. Some nice stuff, actually.

MR WORTH: Oh nice. It's trying to make a bit of a comeback, rep.

MR CHANCERY: Yeah. Nice to get to play a load of different parts.

MR WORTH: What plays you doing?

MR CHANCERY: Some new thing by a local writer, a Pinter, an Agatha Christie and a Shakespeare.

MR WORTH: Oh, which Shakespeare?

MR CHANCERY: *Twelfth Night*.

MR WORTH: OK. Who're you playing?

MR CHANCERY: Andrew Aggycheck.

MR WORTH: Oh course you are. You done any Shakespeare before?

MR CHANCERY: No, not yet.

MR WORTH: Well I suppose *Twelfth Night* is as good a place to start as any. It's flawed, though – the timelines don't make sense.

MR CHANCERY: If you say so.

MR WORTH: I've always wanted to play Hamlet. So complicated – such a brilliant journey.

MR CHANCERY: Bit wordy, though.

MR WORTH: What?

MR CHANCERY: Bit wordy, innit.

MR WORTH: *Hamlet?*

MR CHANCERY: Yeah.

MR WORTH: He's dealing with some of the deepest existential issues that can face a human – battling depression, suppressing rage, grieving. He has some of the best soliloquys in the English language.

MR CHANCERY: Yeah, like I said, wordy.

MR WORTH: You're a charlatan.

MR CHANCERY: And proud of it.

MR WORTH: You'll struggle with it if you've never done Shakespeare before.

MR CHANCERY: Ah, it's all the same – show up, shout a bit, go to the pub. Nobody understands what's going on, anyway, they just pretend to to look intelligent.

MR WORTH: Rubbish.

MR CHANCERY: Fact.

MR WORTH: If the audience doesn't understand what's going on it's because the actors aren't telling the story clearly enough.

MR CHANCERY: What story? It's a load of idiots in silly costumes tarting around.

MR WORTH: I can't talk to you.

ACT THREE

MR CHANCERY: Well, if you're so desperate to do some Shakespeare, tell your agent to get you some.

MR WORTH: Oh yeah, why didn't I think of that?

MR CHANCERY: Have you spoken to them recently?

MR WORTH: My agent?

MR CHANCERY: Yeah.

MR WORTH: Not really.

MR CHANCERY: What do you mean, not really?

MR WORTH: I mean I haven't really spoken to them *re*-cently.

MR CHANCERY: When did you last talk to them?

MR WORTH: Well, we spoke just before tonight's show, if you must know.

MR CHANCERY: And did you tell them you wanted to do some Shakespeare?

MR WORTH: Well no – it didn't... quite come up in conversation, because—

MR CHANCERY: Well, there's your problem, then – they probably don't know!

MR WORTH: They're dropping me.

MR CHANCERY: What?

MR WORTH: That's why they called. They're dropping me.

MR CHANCERY: Oh... well.

MR WORTH: Didn't do a single other job between last year's panto and this one.

MR CHANCERY: I see.

MR WORTH: And they don't feel that our relationship is one that they can see bearing fruit in the future.

(*Pause.*)

MR CHANCERY: That's why you've been so wound up.
MR WORTH: I suppose.
MR CHANCERY: Oh mate, I'm sorry.
MR WORTH: I'll live.
MR CHANCERY: Still, break-ups can be hard.
MR WORTH: It's not a break-up.
MR CHANCERY: Well, it's kind of a break-up.
MR WORTH: It's just the end of a business agreement – that's all. Plenty of actors work without agents.
MR CHANCERY: True. So you're not too upset, then?
MR WORTH: No, course not.
MR CHANCERY: I know it means a lot to you.
MR WORTH: Yeah, well.
MR CHANCERY: I don't think I've met anyone as passionate about this industry as you.
MR WORTH: Thanks.
MR CHANCERY: How long have you been doing it?
MR WORTH: All my life.
MR CHANCERY: That's what they all say.
MR WORTH: Since I was nine.
MR CHANCERY: Nine?
MR WORTH: Yeah.
MR CHANCERY: Nine years old?
MR WORTH: Yeah.
MR CHANCERY: Jesus.
MR WORTH: It's what I've always wanted – what I've dedicated my life to.
MR CHANCERY: Nine years old.
MR WORTH: Yep. It all started with a panto – got the bug.
MR CHANCERY: I see.
MR WORTH: How about you?

ACT THREE

MR CHANCERY: I sort of fell into it after college.

MR WORTH: Fell into it?

MR CHANCERY: Yeah. I just used to spend a lot of time fooling around, and someone suggested my energy could be harnessed in a more productive way. Did a bit of am dram, got an agent and have just been stumbling through since then.

MR WORTH: Right.

MR CHANCERY: Fairly different paths, then.

MR WORTH: You could say that.

MR CHANCERY: But you're genuinely all right?

MR WORTH: Yeah, course.

MR CHANCERY: You sure?

MR WORTH: Of course I'm sure. I've been doing this for twenty-one years.

MR CHANCERY: OK. I mean, I know we have our differences, but I'd hate to see you upset.

MR WORTH: Oh yeah, you've always tried to spare my feelings, haven't you?

MR CHANCERY: What?

MR WORTH: Doesn't matter.

MR CHANCERY: No, go on.

MR WORTH: No, it's nothing.

MR CHANCERY: It's clearly something.

MR WORTH: Just go meet your agent.

MR CHANCERY: No, say what you have to say.

MR WORTH: I shouldn't have said anything. It's fine.

MR CHANCERY: This is about *Babes in the Wood*, isn't it?

MR WORTH: What?

MR CHANCERY: Look, I'm sorry, but it's just the way I am.

MR WORTH: I don't know what you're talking about.

MR CHANCERY: If I'd have known you were going to hang on to it this long then I wouldn't have—
MR WORTH: Stop this!
MR CHANCERY: I didn't mean to hurt you.

(*Long pause.*)

MR WORTH: Yeah, well.
MR CHANCERY: It was a showmance. These things happen.
MR WORTH: Can we not?
MR CHANCERY: I was just out of a long-term relationship – I wasn't in a good place.
MR WORTH: Seems like you're still not in a good place.
MR CHANCERY: I really didn't mean… to hurt you.
MR WORTH: Let's just leave it. Please.

(*Pause.*)

MR CHANCERY: Are you coming back next year?
MR WORTH: Well yeah, I assume so.
MR CHANCERY: You assume so?
MR WORTH: Yeah – they've usually asked by now haven't they?
MR CHANCERY: Erm. I don't know.
MR WORTH: But yeah, if they ask I'll do it. You?
MR CHANCERY: Erm. Yeah. Yeah, same.
MR WORTH: Right.
MR CHANCERY: Yeah.
MR WORTH: Maybe separate dressing rooms next year, though…

ACT THREE

MR CHANCERY: What, and miss out on all the fun?
MR WORTH: Is that what you call it?

(MR CHANCERY *laughs a little. Pause.*)

Was it bad?
MR CHANCERY: Was what bad?
MR WORTH: The song sheet?
MR CHANCERY: Well, it wasn't your finest hour.
MR WORTH: I've never done that before.
MR CHANCERY: No.
MR WORTH: Never done anything like that before.
MR CHANCERY: Well, remember that show when I said we were going to Cinderella's funeral instead of her wedding?
MR WORTH: I called the audience cunts.
MR CHANCERY: Yeah. A bit worse, I suppose.
MR WORTH: They're not asking me back, are they?

(*Long pause.*)

MR CHANCERY: Well, I'd better not keep them waiting any longer.
MR WORTH: Yeah, no, sure. Sorry.
MR CHANCERY: No worries.
MR WORTH: Well. Maybe see you next year.
MR CHANCERY: Yeah… erm, maybe.
MR WORTH: Good luck with the rep season.
MR CHANCERY: Thanks. Good luck with… everything.
MR WORTH: Thanks.
MR CHANCERY: Yeah.

OH NO IT ISN'T!

(*Silence.* MR CHANCERY *leaves* MR WORTH *sitting at his dressing table with a face full of faded, smudged make-up.* MR WORTH *looks at himself in the mirror.*)

MR WORTH: Oh that this too, too sullied flesh would melt thaw and resolve itself into a dew…

(*Lights fade to black.*)

ALSO BY LUKE ADAMSON:

ONE LAST WALTZ

Alice is becoming more and more forgetful. Her daughter Mandy is always on hand to help out, but is starting to feel the strain. One day a long-forgotten photograph stirs a memory and lures Alice back to the Crown Hotel in Blackpool, where she hopes for the chance to dance in the tower ballroom one last time. But when mother and daughter reach Blackpool, nothing is quite how Alice remembers, and she finds herself getting lost in the past.

One Last Waltz is a beautifully written portrayal of a family coming to terms with complications caused by Alzheimer's disease. By turns sparkling with wit and heart-wrenching in its honesty, it's filled with vital and compassionate insight into the sufferings accompanying a disease that has blighted the landscape for so many.

ISBN: 9781804470275 • 72pp • £7.99